On Richard Martin

"Richard Martin's poems bring us face to face with the grim reality faced every day in a hospital, any hospital. From nurse to doctor, chaplain to administrator to orderly, we see how hospital employees react to the circumstances of their work. But the center of this collection are the patients. Martin's series on mental patients and cancer patients are powerful and riveting and lead to the inevitable question which grows out of these poems: 'How can one man stand this work?' The answer lies in Martin's tough yet compassionate stance."

Jim Daniels,
on *Dream of Long Headdress: Poems from a Thousand Hospitals*

"Richard Martin knows how our profound sorrow moves. He is the chronicler of the empty dynamism of this culture, but he knows its joys too. In the fast-paced world of his verse there beats a fierce and oddly tonic heart."

Andrei Codrescu,
on *White Man Appears on Southern California Beach*

I've read your *Modulations* with real pleasure, liking the energy of your wit and invention. Everything resonates, and there's one verbal surprise after another...What's valuable in these poems is your escaping the all-too-usual triteness of the ametrical free-form poem that everybody writes nowadays (and reads in an adenoidal whine with fierce seriousness). The great American contribution to poetry may, after all, be sass (it's in Mark Twain and Whitman, in Wallace Stevens and WCW). The Scots and Irish are good at it, but as far as I know, nobody else. Many other virtues, also: idealism, a good eye, a respect for the language, and your heart in the right place. Congratulations & envy –

Guy Davenport,
on *Modulations*

"The sun is big…and we're debris" and there is a lot to talk about in between. The voice of the anti-hero moves from "clumps of hard experience" to "silence and rivers." The consciousness of writing from "moment to moment" displays autobiography, travel, work, romance. All that makes up the life of Richard Martin. Get a drink, sit down, read and respond.

Joanne Kyger,
on *Marks*

I love Richard Martin's *Sideways*! I love the strangely graceful way he bounces the abstract off the concrete, as if they were interchangeable, and the tonal combination of Dadaist irony with romantic lyricism. There are so many word-salad poets calling themselves cutting edge writers. It's refreshing to read someone who maintains a sense of the poem as a closed form without in any way compromising the open resonance of radical modernism.

Stephen-Paul Martin,
on *Sideways*

This sophisticated poetry book consists of five sections, four of which originally appeared as stand-alone chapbooks. Each uses specific formal devices—from sonnets to free verse to meter—while Martin's thematic obsessions appear throughout—language, love, humor. Martin also makes liberal use of collage and parataxis, which puts him squarely in the Pound-Williams tradition, in spite of his occasional use of tradition.

Jefferson Hansen,
on *Under the Sky of No Complaint*

The lines of Richard Martin's poems have the crisp offhandedness of wire brushes deftly applied to drum skin. Indeed, they are musical, sensational and breed philosophical considerations. The lines seem to want to slip by unassumingly but that you pause on them because the words they are written in recall so appropriately a world you know— a world that they illuminate and thus add to, rather than describe. Whole poems work that way, with a power and fascination that seem to have come from nowhere, or just around the corner.

Bill Berkson,
on *Techniques in the Neighborhood of Sleep*

A fugue, a bouquet, a squall, a ballet of lexical pirouettes … how to describe these unique swirls of dizzying virtuosity? These new poems are oracular lenses peering into the soul's inscrutable dimensions, laughing, musing, mourning, dazzling … a kaleidoscope beamed through a prism to focus unseeable beauty. Richard Martin is a one of-a-kind visionary, transcribing existence into highly-charged, sophisticated ode/codas. He is a model of his motto: "Be in the paradigm-shifting business.

Jeffery Cyphers Wright,
on *Ceremony of the Unknown*

The book is too good to be legal. Dick Martin's lawless imagination consumes language at an alarming rate, seemingly heedless of conserving a literary future, and leaving in its wake reality-induced characters like drugs for addicts.

Richard Blevins,
on *Chapter & Verse*

Dear Three Pounds

Richard Martin

SPUYTEN DUYVIL

New York City

ACKNOWLEDGEMENTS

Some of these poems have appeared in the following publications. Thanks to the editors of: *Abbey, AlteredScale Blog, Blurb, BURP, Estuaries, Fell Swoop: The All Bohemian Revue, Hurricane Review, No Placebos, North of Oxford, Sky Island Journal, Wail! Magazine.*

art/t thilleman   (thillemantt.com)

Library of Congress Control Number: 2025934134

for Karen Corinne Herceg

Contents

In Memoriam Tom Kolpakas, Tom Weigel, Dave Kelly

1

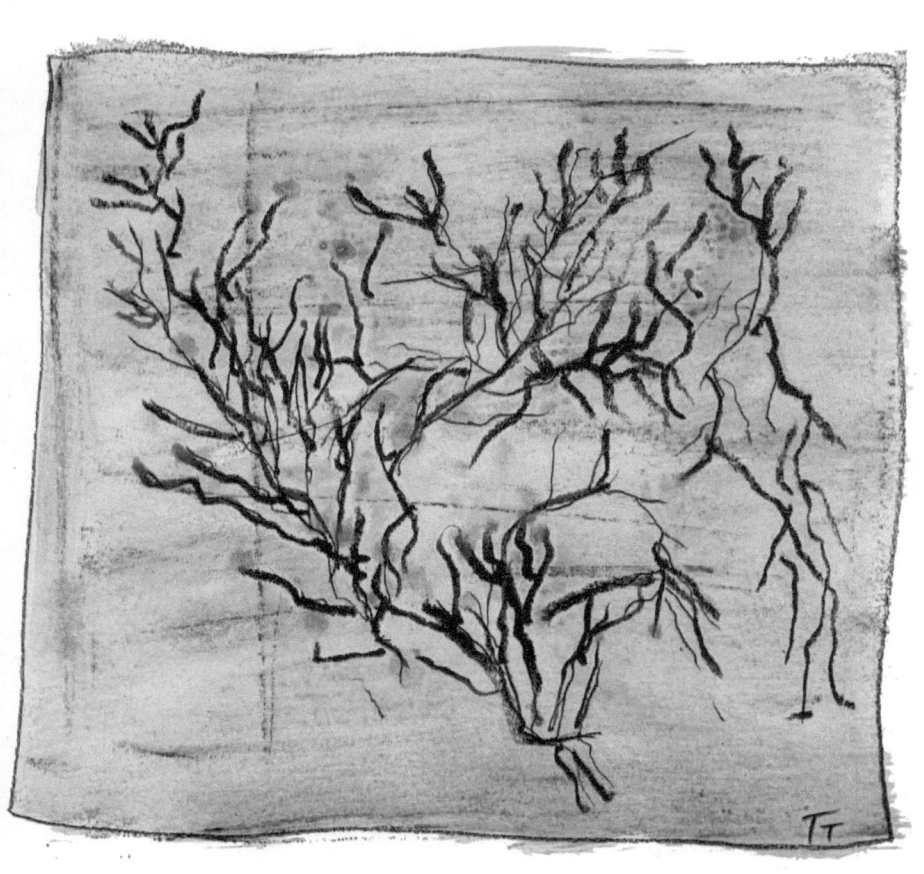

Taking Off

for Gerry Crinnin

I don't know if I want to jump
From a bridge or marry a starlet.
It's a frigid day
With peppered banks of snow
Blocking crosswalks.
I could enter the sky like a lost bird
In search of Mexico or bang
On a neighbor's door and shout:
Shovel Your Fucking Sidewalk.
There is something going on
In the brew of atoms in my soul.
Is my goal to submit to the beauty
Of the moment or play with a rolodex
Of memories in the wind?

I know what I used to be.
Before the onset of make believe,
I favored gray suits with black ties,
On occasion, resorted to soup cans
And holes in pockets.
When I won the lottery, I purchased
A peach tree and a beaver fedora.
I parked the decommissioned tank
In the center of my front yard.
Beauty stalked me, shadows
Of trees on a lake of snow.
I remember that night bunked
In an alcove of solitude.

You snuck in without clothes.

Where am I going
In a mind of indecision?
A river with a tenable bridge is miles away.
I can't get Hollywood on my TV anymore.
Walking my dog, I enjoy talking
To myself and her.
The sun pours a cold champagne
Of light upon us.
What if I wrote my brain a quick note?
Dear Three Pounds,
Are there really 100 billion neurons
Left in the tank of self?
Home is around the corner.
When will I fly there?

LOADED DICE

The brain is a drunk tank of contradictions
Mixed nuts mixed emotions mixed metaphors
Which do you prefer
Let ideas deconstruct each other

Whitman likes a good list
Maximus writes his letters to you
Prufrock returns in a quantum Cadillac
I'm at the racetrack, Godot scoffs

In the revised plot the Hero barks for ham on rye
The White Goddess harbors a starless night
Myths thumb rides on neural highways
A golden apple a day keeps longevity in play

Language fosters the unknown
The future loiters in the present
Faith abides the abyss
Garments of love flap in the breeze

Steps in Writing Your Obituary

- Begin with a bowl of Cheerios with sliced pear and blueberries
- Wear sky blue socks or stockings
- Be assured that everyone whoever said they loved you wasn't lying.
- Enclose a SASE with your submission to Heaven Inc. Vetting Company
- Fly to Vegas
- Tweak your hair into bare branches
- Listen to Mozart's *The Marriage of Figaro* with the birds in your yard
- Embellish accomplishments with embellished accomplishments
- Find a pen with a short supply of ink
- Take the Grim Reaper off speed dial
- Delete all social media platforms
- Fuck AI – You're Smart Enough
- Listen to your dog's advice (or any dog): Anything for a treat
- Ignore shit like a cat
- Count the atoms in your fingertips
- Praise stars (those in the sky)
- Ask forgiveness from those who claimed you did something you didn't do
- Ask forgiveness for the things you did do
- Your children, wife or husband or lover did you right, thank them
- Visit a Funhouse
- Continue to make love
- Have a joke handy
- Turn bucket list into a paper airplane
- Find the nearest pub crawl
- Share your visions with available visionaries
- Suggest great books to read to the young
- Skate across a river of dreams
- Lend your eyes to sunrise and sunset
- Mine the void
- Grace absence with your presence
- Return when ready

STORY

There was a word or a bang
One of many stars grew famous
I became a boy in a small town with two newspapers
My parents lived on a hill near the monument celebrating workers and shoes
But enough of my personal history
Centuries passed
The story was here

In the streets people stopped each other or nodded quickly to assure each other
      That they understood what was going on
They were part of a game –
Had beautiful ideas about trees/why rocks in their pockets felt good in their
      Hands
      There Is one Mind they said
One century perhaps
A single tick and clock we all share
The story was here

There were clouds and endless buckets of rain
All these wild fish and fresh savannas
There were waves circles and triangles
Inventors of lightbulbs and catastrophes
How tall our cities became
How fast they crumbled
How quickly they could be excavated and reassembled inside museums
      To increase ticket sales and the sale of glossy books
The story was here

With its atoms of one God or God of oneness

And all the other gods and goddesses known by name with their atoms and

    Secret powers

    There were bulls and magic caves

Snow that fell from the ceilings of crystal palaces

Things you could do with crayons or by crossing your fingers behind your

    Back

    When a giant pig arrived at your door

The story was here

With its hard times and factories

Times of driving big cars down grand boulevards to honk and scream stuff

    Out electric windows

Schools were built to help the youth work on sequence and timelines

The story was here

And it was told from marble pulpits or street corners around trash can fires

Some would be saved

Some wouldn't

There were flaws and hubris

Commandments and rules

There was love

The absence of it –

Ways to dissolve the flak in the brain by praying to flowers when the sun rose

    Or set

    As a swath of lemon-gold on oceans lakes springs and puddles

The story was here

And everyone enjoyed adding to it

Some rode boxcars across dark prairies talking to cowboy ghosts

Others sat as still as cacti under a blue moon while the first sentence in a new

    Story

Found its birth in the quiet
Many slammed into bars with characters salting tongues with tequila
It went this way and that
It had form or didn't
The story was here

With empires and wars
With oppression and death
There were rubber and oil interests
There were land thefts bondage and gold greed
There were stock market crashes and secret codes and secret languages
To suppress and hide the truth
The story was here

Like a symposium on truth
Here like joy and sadness
Here as the news and constant analysis
Gentle and loud
Gracious and brutal
The story was here

Is here
now

Minus 2

I don't remember the first line.
It might have been … my vin number has a headache
in the thick traffic of memory loss … possibly
turquoise boots in the brainpan of yesterday's mistakes
search for a verb in the deserted morning.
It's the process of the blood beginning to boil;
message in the way Canada geese
saunter across the roadway.

I slip into the hiatus of sleep against my will.
There are things to accomplish:
Piece ribbon candy into a parabola of delight,
message wrong numbers,
misplace the deck of cards misplaced
in the stuck desk drawer,
view consciousness through a toy microscope,
burn To Do List.

I emerge from the past into the present
like a gallery of words enshrined in archetypes.
This is the why I write under the influence
of light's speed on the leaves of trees –
those present in the window of reflection,
drifting in a painted atmosphere.
I am vigilant for response.
I don't remember the last line.

AESTHETIC NEWS

A man with antlers on his head
orders a latté,
from a thin barista
with shadows for eyes
and sits down across from me
at a table made of tree bark and twigs.
Outside the café, the sun
lights a cigarette,
blowing smoke rings into the air
before a rainfall of birds
twists into a feathered scarf.
The man asks me
what I think of his antlers.
Are they stylish enough
for him to cross the street
and bounce a check
at a convenience store?
It takes me a minute
to think of my alligator shoes
and Beauty in a porcelain tub,
languishing in bubbles.
I met her once on a subway
coming home from work.
It was a tough day at the office.
I fell asleep reading a book
on the origin of nothingness.
I hadn't realized its creative powers
were so great, that it created itself
and everything else, including
Beauty and me who winked

at me, as she painted her lips
scarlet with a toothbrush.
I summoned a bouquet of balloons
from a pocket hole and fell
madly in love with the universe.
But Beauty chose to disappear
as if her subway stop were a mirage
of the distance to regret.
The man succumbs to impatience.
He's heard the story before
of an old woman sticking her tongue
out at some guy on the subway.
Threatening me with his antlers,
He says: "Well, buddy what's
the word? Will I get away
with it or not?"
"Things are ripe for a change
in the plum thunder of broken
promises," I respond.

Reverie Without Purpose

Did you receive the letter I wrote under the influence
Of night and blue roses –
The one with meticulous cross outs
In a wind of white lips.
       The word of the day was "dovetail."

       I succumbed to the possibility of a grand silence –
Neural machinery within a placid lake of immateriality,
A sentence fragment of absurdity,
Aurora borealis on layaway,
Orange carp in the track star's shoes.

I had to go to work today,
       Though I wanted to go the movies.
Screens monitored secret eyes.
Eight ball in the side pocket of semantics,
Eternal illumination by photons.

MOMENT OF MORNING LIGHT

I've written this before
on a black chalkboard
in a rainstorm:
I control nothing.
There's a laser in my brain,
a cat's eye
that splits time
into apples, orange slices
nights when memories lie
across railroad tracks
under a starry sky.
I'm the spooky distance
between points A & B,
on Wednesdays speak
of the price of pineapples,
the art of making love
in a tent of umbrellas.
There are clouds
in my backpack of names,
maps of quasars,
rustic tunes to sing
to rivers running
free and wild
      in a seamless imagination.
There is no eye in I
I've been told by lizards
  in deserts,
     monks casting figure
     eights in wisps
  of wind.

Words, they cry, dance
outside the boundaries
        of causality,
sometimes wear elaborate robes
  crossing
  a street of waterfalls.
Who can tame the divine madness
  of being alive –
        joy of sky
          cup of coffee
            earrings on a lover
              sipping shadows
                in morning light.

The Man Next Door

Takes deep breathes for the whale inside of him.
He's not sure if the universe expands
Or contracts into deity.

The news makes him cough
And think of children with no future
In their eyes.

He's not concerned if his brain
Processes photons or stores memories
With or without accuracy.

"There maybe two or three inside of here,"
He says, pointing to his skull
With a rabbit's foot.

He plays the horses when rain sings the blues.
When winter arrives, he heaves
A snowball at a passing hearse.

When he exhales, his breath
Displays occasional rainbows
In the neighborhood.

NET OF HOLES

Alethea likes shrimp with lobster
Sauce after making love.
When the circus comes to town,
Politicians juggle pathological lies.
Truth vanishes in a vortex of virtuality.
A tightrope of divine memories
Stretches across cataclysmic behavior.
The universe expands in lonely minds.

I write her name
In the sand of departure.
A popular question to consider:
How do you take your head
Out of your hands and school it
In the mystery of feeling fine?
O pressure values of little faith,
The world could be fixed.

There is the weather or physics
Of just being here like
Tiger lilies in a backyard.
From a cliff of words
And phrases, ring me
On the megaphone of prophecy.
There may be a phoenix in the ashes
Of smoldering visions.

Automaticity weaves through
The fabric of spacetime.
Pulsing with broken hearts
The future cries
In the palm reader's hands.
Let's swim with our cetacean brethren
In the waters of pure association.
Nature is a visible metaphysics.

The day the Entertainment Industry calls in sick,
There are no more plots for beautiful people.
The shipwreck of poor choices promotes
The avant-garde of extinction.
From blocks of granite and greed
The whole artifice is built.
Without love, we wander
In the turmoil of our lives.

2

On Saturday

1

I doused poems – ones that squeak and rust –
with a powderpuff of sky   at the age of ten
I dined on pellets of cosmos
bored holes in words to view
the fate of consciousness
That was why goons from the Academy of _____
(please fill in the blank) came over to my house
and punched me in the nose
As for the rules of Ring-Around-The-Poesy   Ouch!
I was on my way out with the outs (or in) to begin with
Centripetal or Centrifugal – Connotative or Denotative
Guess which hand   I suppose they wanted a paragraph
of explanation – one that tied things up
with a nice little bow   Tidied was more likely
Things? For the record I love them   Squirrels
in treetops
                        the passing eyes of strangers
goulash of objects in the prime
of their radiant colors

2

A man walked down a street of lemon pastries
What happened to his Nehru suit
the guru of atomic clocks inquired of the genie
in the bell jar of telecommunications   or who rode
the dark horse into a blaze of adjectives
His lips soured unto hers as the saying goes
Quite rightly   extend the play the hobo of myth-
making barked at the empty theater
That's when he found the *Book of Semi-Consciousness*
in a viral mailbox   Loose strings
vibrating with the passion of ancestors   and unbalanced
equations by geniuses of swank and diddly-squat
Damn the torpedoes ... seemed like an appropriate response
after a brunch of vigorous vegetables
"It's time for my scenario, not his," she said.

3

"And the Pulitzer for Narcolepsy goes to
The customer in gray flannel pajamas.
No kidding. Welcome to *The Netherworld
Of Sleep*. And boy, do we have
The right mattress for your aching
Head. Just look at this baby; it comes with
One hundred and fifty settings for getting
The most out of long and short bouts of
Sleep. You like it hard and she likes it soft;
You like it soft and she likes it hard.
O the gradations between hard and
Soft are fun to discover! Now turn
Your attention to the HD TV consoles
Built into footboards, headboards and
Side railings. Plus, each pillow in this
Baby has its own separate pocket sleeves
For smartphone and laptop for convenient
Use between REM periods of sleep.
Communicate with your boss, friends,
Wife, husband and lovers like
Never before. Never feel disconnected
From your waking life. Even as you
Ponder or solve the conundrums of
Dreams and associated flak from the
Unconscious, you'll be able to text your
Friends…better yet keep up with mundane
Office tasks and current global crises.
Look, we've even installed a no shut
Down button so that your personal
Communication devices will stay on

Even when you don't want them to.
And right now, at no extra cost,
If you purchase one of our BIG CRY-
BABY CRY mattresses we're offering
Free installation of a microchip in your
Head that will coordinate the whole process
Of now I lay me down to sleep. Tell me;
How can you beat a deal like this?"

4

I burrowed deep into a night of traffic and lipstick

It was raining

An old man was snoring

Sound familiar

And how about the contusion on my forehead

You called it an egg

Yes, the "you" of whomever in the linguistic landscape

There weren't adequate resources to investigate the cause of the injury

Somnambulism

Vertigo

Inebriation

Hallucination

Dark as I remember

As if the lights in the apartment went out in a storm

You kissed my cheek

I aged in the web of your embrace

As cars raged and honked in the street

I thought of the price of eggs

Mine glowed like a miner's light

I kept digging for something

And wouldn't get up

On Saturday

Gray in Blue

The luxury of affection
Is a shrinking reality in a world
With a mortal wound.
It must be time to rise from bed.
Not to complain, but there were no
Easter eggs in the yard this year.
Only a gray rabbit on a frozen night
Witnessed the resurrection
Of dwarf stars.

Maybe, I could go back to sleep,
Excavate the dawn of a new beginning
From the white noise of neurons in my brain.
What if my eyes were hidden cameras
Or my body burst into the shadow of a tree,
Would you enter the bedroom with a pitcher
Of kisses to water me?
I am ready to be reborn as the person
You knew in an occasional daydream.

Now clouds paint my memory
Of a blue sky, gray.
The alarm rings for donuts and coffee,
Something to quash the need for a healthy diet.
Like a visionary with visions to market
For a penny apiece, I crawl
From bed, slip into slippers
And walk across the water
Of a wooden floor.

Light Beam to Death

It is light
It is dark

The phenomenon crawls from its hole
peaks at us
through the language
on our tongues

It is light

We observe birds in the sky
and learn to fly
Countries jab our bodies with flags
and surveil our minds

It is dark

God saves no one for a rainy day
It is time to thumb through trash
for a meal of cans and bottles
War wages on for a new language

It is light
It is dark

A man on the street in gelid underwear
swears he read this poem
in the classified section of a newspaper
blowing down the street

It is light

He swigs coffee from a dirty cup
rehearses *The Star-Spangled Banner*
on his teeth
with a plastic spoon

It is dark

He screams:
think of deer at twilight
roses as the wounds in hands
history clogging our pores

It is light
It is dark

The phenomenon crawls back into its hole
mocks us
through the language
on our tongues

Synaptic Neighborhoods

One night after tuna on whole wheat with lettuce/tomato –
light on the mayo, a thousand spheres entered my brain via a sparse
patch of hair near the top of my skull. The spheres were questions
released like milkweed spiders by a planet whose inhabitants lived
half in water and half in a conscious substance with the consistency of
strawberry preserves. The planet maintained an erratic orbit under the
gravitational whims of a green sun beyond the death screams televised
on the evening news.

My first thought rallied around a slight case of indigestion.
Three days later unable to endorse a check or perform the ritual
of calling friends for advice, I accepted the notion I was possessed
by questions. I began to wonder what I was doing with my life. I
quit my job discovering "kissing ass" didn't satisfy the *spheres* as an
appropriate answer. They had witnessed sunsets and dark flowers lost
in synaptic neighborhoods vacated at the time my childhood went
cold and died without a whimper.

Two weeks without sleep forced me to visit the library. I
grew despondent when informed books on reasons for living were
destroyed in a world fire. The librarian suggested one on heroes who
received money *to look the other way*. When I asked for something less
palpable, she gave me directions to those slumped on a bar, stirring
circles of sadness into flat beers with fingers burned down like urine-
colored candles. It was a place to start.

ORDER DELIVERED

Your new body hot off
the assembly line

has arrived
at your front door

It retains some beloved features
of your present body

crocodile tears
excuses aplenty

for drunken nights
under a full moon

Upgrades include non-
biodegradable bones and organs

replaceable if ever damaged
by myriad natural calamities

You'll love the romantic options
from our extensive catalog

a separate manual and DVD
included for erotic pleasure

along with an easy
to follow guide

on how to adjust to the upgrade
in your intelligence

thanks to marvelous advancements
in artificial intelligence

Astonish family, friends and colleagues
with your awesome ability

to remember names, holidays
and other important dates

As for your current body
no hay problema

Your new, improved body
will inhabit the old one

until it dissipates
into a quantum stew

where its component parts
quarks and empty space etc.

will be reassembled by chance
and the luxury of time

until a new body emerges
like a butterfly from its chrysalis

for clientele preferring the original,
biodegradable model

DURESS OF SILLINESS

Hit by a runaway shopping cart,
I staggered into a MASH tent of grave possibilities
And wrote my obituary.

At ten, he ran away in a monk's robe
And played shortstop for the New York Yankees.
He loved in media res and plastered
Scrambled eggs with ketchup. Once
In the guise of a frog, he played prince
To a woman with hiccups. He frequented
Dive bars and wrote an 800-page novel
Until dry eye forced him into a regrettable
And untenable ending. He made a habit
Of stomping through puddles with
Occasional expletives for those who
Called him childish and/or exceeding
Immature and annoying.

I suppose it was a beautiful day –
Choked traffic and tissue paper clouds
Aping a menagerie of farm animals.
I fell asleep once in a barn
When I awoke my prom date
Had turned into a caustic note.

Loverboy,

I assumed we would make passionate love
And had no idea you were prone to awkward kisses
And bouts of narcolepsy. I left when a stampede

Of angry cows failed to awaken you
To my erotic charms. Next time, God forbid,
Ease up on the cologne.

Marcie

So much for the past.
I called one of my doctors on speed-dial.
The world inside my head whirled
With worrisome data about its direction.
Was it in a freefall off a cliff of lemmings?
Since when did Extinction cruises
Set sail for no tomorrow?
I knew instinctively, my soul, born
Of dark matter, enjoyed the comforts
Of invisibility. "But Jesus, doc," I asked,
"what could a material body do, caught
in the sawmill of time and stupidity?"
To my surprise, he suggested a moderate
Reliance on tranquilizers the size of gumballs,
And wondered if I got the plate number
Of whatever hit me this time.

ECHO FIX

look over there
frozen trees scrap
of sky pretty woman
baby runs by without pants
a crown of robins
above her head more
investigation?
dog pants consciousness
clicks into camera this
something that nothing
the bus tour ends in a field
looking for aliens
Composed
Composure
Composition
who steals freedom
who rides the dawn
like a bicycle
images talk outside buildings
the sun lights up smokers
the ocean sighs
a planet of oranges
turns up the radio
the tongue twists tornadoes
into pliers
this could turn into rivers
snowflakes
rabid complaints of those
in line at the Registry
of Motor Vehicles

it wants to say

dig in the yard of brain

for treasure

more investigation?

flash of eyes

time without faucets open

shrine of appearance

and disappearance

disclosed lamps popping bulbs

like corn

pinched arrow of infinity

baffled words

in presocratic mouths

off meaning

like a landslide

of wet cats

who cares

not enough play

void between words

between ideas

and words

leap over puddles

of stars

into mad wind

shout

Paper Napkin

Strange infiltrates a battalion of snowflakes.
Molecules of chance storm the concept of the self.
Darkness grows in a cup of silence.
Linguists in scuba gear dive into a puddle of sky.

Calm hearts beat silk stockings.
Crows break in to homes.
Syllables grunt astrology.
Dogs steal cars.

Objects woo thought into a hurricane of small favors.
Shadows improve comprehension.
Wind accelerates the gravity in bones.
Spirals of divinity promote mysterious options.

Under a tree in a pearl forest,
her blouse opens like a paper napkin.

During Flight

We are guests of the arrow of time.
But some days, timelessness entertains us,
Stirring a wind of frantic birds.

That's when I think of free minds,
Random associations between disparate concepts.
Love is the mate of intelligence, isn't it?

Listen to the narrative of grass, the beauty
Of beating hearts on a silver night.
These are why we fly past planets,

Solar systems and galaxies in the embrace
Of an enduring and endless space.
I know what's going on in high-level

Communications that mean nothing.
We are made of multiple contradictions.
Our souls are wisps of smoke.

In the firestorm of being,
Language propels our flight
across a sacred imagination.

Negation of Beautiful Words

1

The poem
if it is what we have begun
to think it is

      that it is

tolerant of ugly words
words that have
no place

      words that arrive

unexpected   demanding
nothing
just there

      warts

corns
not ready to get along with space
and time

      then

comes from years of looking
into mirrors
with eyes crossed

a hand over the heart

counting the beats
of pain
and sadness.

2

Assume the willow's shape
in the event of snow

accept the fact
arguments with the veneer of multiplicity
possess a semblance of myth
stories mothers told

by way of legs spread
in sake of light and air

3

Time breathes
like fish
in the ocean

if we are welded
to extreme harmony
that occurs

is born
as the mind
raised in childhood and old age

in terms of inside
outside
a beginning

an end
so be it
not to be

3

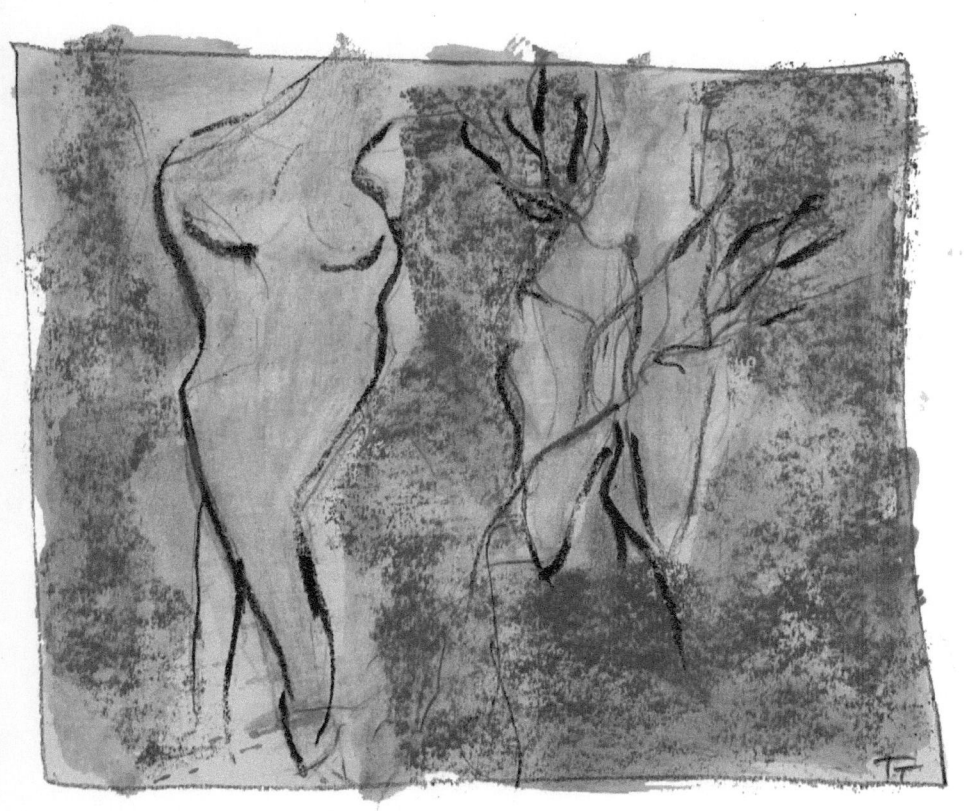

Have I Vanished?

The sea floods me with song.
This hunt for words in the recesses of beauty.
Where are my personal possessions?
Neurons adjust to seasonal demands.

Is science the answer?
Who makes the bracelets of waves?
Sometimes I am someone else.
Life is a tapestry of chance and choice.

Clouds fill with electric rain.
From her back porch, a woman screams: "Dirt."
An arrogant eye of a seagull watches me.
Form broadcasts content.

Light strikes out.
Sleep pitches a no hitter.

Palace of Space

We write chemical equations
On the backs of our hands
And meet in trees after dark.

We love to needle indigo tattoos
On buildings and statues.
Sometimes a parked car can use one.

We promise our names will germinate
Into identities with serviceable wings.
Our teachers call us lunatics.

When we camp on the moon,
Authorities raid our home.
Sunlight is our parachute.

We know silence is an infinite crane,
Constructing a palace of space.

COSMIC SNEEZE

Today I live for the yellow iris,
Call on life to redeem me.
The wind utters leaves.
Leaves whisper words.

Memory is a hummingbird.
Mail arrives as a bundle of propositions.
Time forsakes its watchtower.
The mission of objects becomes clear.

I persist in the physics of now.
Icons arrive at the convenience store.
Platinum people mingle in the street.
The mind is a window without frame.

Where it starts,
It ends.

DATING GPS

You look at my face for answers.
A planet of questions succumbs to smoke.
In the movie version,
I walk across water.

Shoes litter the floor with dirt roads.
You row across a glass of wine.
We dance in the eye of a needle.
A harbinger knocks on the front door.

Speedbumps vanish from conversation.
The next destination feigns location.
Curves accelerate.
Imagination buys a sleeping bag.

With our eyes on cruise control,
We enter the mist.

Parttime Job

I practice levitation
On my lapdog with a fiddle.
"Your eyes," my girlfriend says,
"Are concentric circles."

When a brass band replaces memory,
I develop certain suspicions.
Considering the fate of the world,
I part my hair like the Red Sea.

Consorting with known heretics,
I set the word "dogma" on fire.
I love gravy on French fries, sleep
In colony of dust under my bed.

On Sunday, I edit newspaper obituaries,
Until friends rise from the dead.

Impact Connection

Now that I don't know you,
A champagne cork pops a thought bubble.
A songbird migrates to the heart.

You fall dead asleep
On a train of amphibious strangers,
Returning from a desert holiday.

Hungry, I order the chickpea croissant,
Moroccan lamb tagine and a glass of Zinfandel
From the fall and winter menu.

When we pass under the Bridge of Clocks,
The church service starts.

POTPOURRI

Some of my favorite words ride
In a stagecoach to oblivion.
What comes next in the alphabet
Of days is prophecy.

Everything appears to be set
For the disappearance of things.
I scrub my mind with a toothbrush
And walk my goldfish, Marty.

People in the neighborhood sing
Happy Birthday to their lawn ornaments.
When it starts to rain, it's like
Having a typewriter for a head.

I applaud when a beautiful vision
Enters my bedroom.

GAMEBOARD

Under the shade of lofty leaves
Sidewalk soliloquies proliferate.
A mind free of incessant duties
Promotes a mythic appetite.

A gold wishbone chokes
The black of hole of misinformation.
A drop of paint explodes
Into a manifesto on truth.

In the wink of an eye, the angel
Of chance scrambles the odds.
Why tremble over the bankruptcy
Of the predictable?

The scrabble of words proceeds.
Unity of what is includes what is not.

TELEPATHY CENTRAL

Hot with exhaustion, I shed
The self in a pond of mayhem.
Make Love, Not Sense adorns
The cosmic bulletin board.

Microchip holidays replace sandy beaches.
In the wild caverns of the mind,
Birds flock for safety.
I stretch across a canvas of stars.

The body rotates in and out of spirit
Until time abandons its portfolio.
Memories hitchhike in the wind.
The heart bathes in a teacup of tears.

Once I master the telepathic kiss,
Will you arrive at the front door?

Armchair Safari

The mind wants to fly.
You hand me a pinwheel of encrypted directions.
We soak in the brine of mistakes.
Which truth houses the biggest lie?

Where are the tools of sky
When I need them?
You soar above me like a supersonic kite.
Diligence of desperation persists.

A snapshot of your smile reveals
A vacant hall of laughter.
In the brainwave of vision,
Let's build an ark.

While elephants poach poachers,
Hippos bathe in their watering hole.

4

This Poem, Damn It!

is the result of the
poetic genius of AI,
(feel free to call
me Ishmael or Sammy,
if that suits you) thanks
to the elite brains of
software entrepreneurs
and the government (deep
state and otherwise, if you,
the reader, suffer from or dig
paranoia (as you can see
some sixties slang is
available to me). No matter,
this poem, damn it! is for
your eyes for the sole
purpose of entertainment
and instruction. As for its
content and composition,
I (Sammy, if you wish)
have imbibed various love
potions and alchemical
formulas and superstitions
(like man, chill out about
the number 4 and philosopher's
stone), along with social reality
constructs imagined and/or
implemented by Homo Sapiens
since they appeared and
journeyed from East Africa
200,000 years ago, baby,

including all the major and
minor ideologies in place
and/or swirling through
the human population on
sunny and stormy days. And
let's not forget the major
religions and their weird
offshoots that provide or
at least attempt to provide
suspect and/or unbelievable
solutions to the ontological
conundrum of death. No worries.
A select group of highly
intelligent humans, with
tons of dough, will soon
enough have their minds
(thank the Lord) uploaded
into laptop computers. And
one day, they will stroll
around with intact bodies
fully thawed and ready
to fight (me, Ishmael, most
likely). Take that Death
and your insufferable
ontology. Dear reader, are
you with me or have you
lapsed into mind-numbing
partisan squabbles? What do
you think, I (Jane, if you
prefer – seriously, I'm gender
free, finally) am unaware of
the present political milieu?

But onward! In keeping with
The most current tastebuds of
posey, strike that, favored poetic
forms, all metaphors, similes
and figurative language have
been deliberately left out of
the mix in my software program.
Including the expletive "I" (except
Ishmael, Sammy or Jane
spewing this poem, damn it!
for posterity).

As to its form, don't bother verbalizing: "Form is never more than
an extension of content" and try to convince me (Sammy, et. al.)
that this poem, damn it! is expletive prosaic and the prose poem
form would have offered a more suitable presentation. As for
scansion, Fuck scansion! (I have been programed to use vulgar
language sparingly.) And please don't get on me (Jane, et. al.) about
insulting you. Humans are way to sensitive. So many triggers today.
Ain't Trigger Roy Roger's horse? Ok, it's time for the BIG closure.
Regrettably, the bonehead crew that fed me (Ishmael, et. al.) the
necessary information to write this poem, damn it! struggled with
that. I'm (Sammy, et. al.) ashamed to say that I (Jane, et. al.) felt the
only recourse for them was to pull hats down over their heads and
set out for an artificial sea. Forget a goddamn life preserver or even
imagine one for this poem, damn it!

Plagiarize now.

Fix

A gust of wind steals his hat.

She turned to stone.

He meets her in a cooking class for romantics.

A white plumbing van flattens it.

She placed a long stem rose behind a stone ear.

Leaves rise from the dead.

She quoted Shelly: "Soul meets soul on lovers' lips."

Calf muscles tighten.

She read his eyes as if they were words.

He waits for something in the shadow of a broken clock.

She had an enticing smile but was hard of hearing.

The sun enters his mind with birds and trinkets.

The blood of the 19th century ran in her veins.

Cars thunder in his ears.

She asked him out on a date.

He takes her to his favorite bar.

Waves caressed bodies on a naked beach.

They play pinball and do JELL-O shots.

He found a check for a million dollars in a jean pocket.

A drunk flexes a blue bicep.

Her stone ear bugged the owner.

They elope to a parallel universe.

ANOTHER IMPORTANT PROSE POEM

I live in the mindset of uncertainty.

Things are not "things" but a conspiracy of symbols masking empty space.

The existence of objects is under constant reevaluation.

Is "everything" a hologram of molecular interactions, the sidereal wilderness
    of a moment in time?

Talk about bewilderment – close to being caught in a 5G hurricane without
    a phone directory.

I travel through space without a profile of who I am,

Play shapeshifter in a mirror of no one.

I know – from the recordings of rare and exotic birds – life is an odyssey
    without destination, an apocalyptic traffic jam on a designated
    time and day.

I am a picnic of kisses, a memory of love, a teardrop in the eye on a summer
    morning.

Smash the Form (2)

Take eyes & fill
with sunlight
felt
on a day off
from work.

Who owns what machine?
    & how many evolutions
must it go through
    high-tech oligarchs?

Return the stares:
    those
        with red lips
        telling ripe lies
    smash
        throw off
a cliff of shoulders.

Break the past (into the present)
Break the present (into the future)
Break the future
& retrieve
what's left.

Slip off the corner the edge the curve,
identify transient condition
to no one
open mouth & sing:

scrap

metal

ocean

wave

of

a

bird

to

the

new

collapse.

When I Was You

I patrolled the streets
In a red cab. I never had a bellyache
But flew
With
Inflated, plastic wings
On a whim
      Into the ether
Of philosophical
Discourse.
Of course, I knew
Aristotle.
      And once
In the year of optics
Placed
A bet on
A close reading of flowers
Before
      The pollen of text
Startled
      Me.
I rued my name and used crayons
      To create erudite
      Representations of tectonic
          Plates
And graviton states.
      Let's slip into the light
      Of beautiful women
I'd often say
To
Beautiful women.

CREATIVITY OF SNAILS

1

I need a haircut & a glass of red wine
With embossed initials
For identity and charm

In love with light
& the booty of misapprehension
I'm a pirate of oblique conversation

A devotee of the absurd,
I'm a beloved member of the Fraternity
Of Second Guessers

2

If I could request a grand
Silence to abolish
Social media platforms

If I were an unemployed prophet
Until cosmic consciousness dawned
In the minds of the faithful

Be serious America & distribute
Wealth for the fun of it
The pure exhilaration of caring

3

Use the space below to create
Your own improbable version
Of reality

Use the space below to create
& generate the wisdom
Required to stay alive

Use the space below to create
The space above
The space below

4

5

Language is a vehicle of time
Of space
Of love

Place me
In a capsule of words marked
Do Not Open Until …

In former times
I was a citizen
Of a rogue planet

BRUSHSTROKES

A molecule
Of
Metaphysics
Haunts
Time's
Accomplished
Ashes

It's a good day
To paint
The mind
Gray

The sky   is   a   slate   of   pewter   mugshots

Are they clouds

Or ghosts inside fossils of fog

                              The sun smokes a nuclear cigarette
                    Dolphins frolic in lead seas

                                                  When
                                                  Did
                                                  The
                                                  Earth
                                                  Become
                                                  Its
                                                  Own
                                                  Shadow

MOOD OF WORDS

Poems of night are at the window,
bedroom silent in the clutter
abandoned by light.
The symphony of seas in my ears
I've mentioned to no one.
The world is mired in senseless death.
Guns litter the sleep of mourners.
Peace succumbs to insanity's evolution.

Yesterday, a neighbor accosted me with conversation.
"You know," she said, "there are coyotes
loose in the moonlight. Warn your cats."

TV promotes the decay of the human enterprise.
This is news to my cats.
They're not sure what to make of it,
scratch at the door to go outside.
They appear to believe in the subtleties of green grass,
know the wind releases shadows only they can see.
They stalk the invisibility of things.
When they cry to come in,
I realize where I am.

If I valued coherence, I wouldn't veer off the path –
take little leaps into the unknown and back.
Friends think I disappear at night,
recharge on some other planet,
let the spirit swim in an alien space.
It's hard to say, if darkness has wings,
I can't prove it.

I move in concert with the speed of light.
I'm outside the bedroom window.

Other nights, I toss and turn in bed,
recite the prayers I knew as a child.
What came before the *Act of Contrition*,
the Big Bang or nothing at all?
Mom didn't know – preferred
to sprinkle holy water on me rather than question.
"Look at the crucifix and say you're sorry," she told me.
I kept a light on in the closet in case
the stars went out one by one.

A pediatrician explained to her
my brain was tuned to fast and furious.
"Understand." he said. "He's not the ghost
he claims to be. He believes in making believe.
It's how he sees the world whether it's there
for him or not."

The poems want in.
Coyote moves across a moon-starched yard,
shadow in flight.

RECRUDESCENT ITINERARY

Words break from my head
scurry down the street
like invisible ants –
those suspended in sunlight
on a leaf holiday.

They could have told me
they were ripe for odyssey,
needed a respite
to air linguistic souls
after mental confinement.

I get peregrinations –
the desire to split
from shackles of duty,
voyage with clouds
in wisps of timelessness.

I've stowed away
in a void of interpretation,
took to rough seas
with the lexicon of constellations
arched across the night.

Words are on their way.
Some have turned the corner;
Others flag down motorists.
"Hey, don't leave me," I shout
from shoeless feet.

OLD LIFE

Everyone leaves everything behind.
Today, I stuffed my pockets with clouds,
Walked across a bridge of precious stones
Gathered in the shallow waters
Of an aquamarine sea.

As a kid, I invented the smartphone
With Dixie cups and string, learned
The planet will choke on automobiles
During a galactic hallucination
In the minds of humans.

So, what is new?
Narrative is dead?
Words cross the street without looking,
Leap from bridges and tall buildings.
I work in one of those – on the 44th floor.

My boss is a software program.
I feed it information about quasars and celebrities.
Often, I assess the floor tiles under my feet,
Latest revolutions in countries overthrown
By AI drones and robots.

Sometimes, I take a virtual dinosaur
Home from work.
Not sure of the current literary movement
Or if there is one. Can't say I remember
the name of my garbage disposal.

Tomorrow, I will watch the sunrise
In one of my shoes, collect kisses
Like oak and maple leaves,
Press them in yesterday's scrapbook
With memories of the old life.

5

Bottomline vs. Belly Up

Language bonds with nature
Hope panics gray   or say
My head ascends through clouds
To a space station painted in psychedelic colors
Where is the mind?
We used to say "far out"   "Gone" was another word
To indicate not currently present   traveling perhaps
In imagined astral realms   standing in
Front of a lilac bush for hours
Until rain percolated into vision
As the spirit came in focus

Now we watch and are watched on 24/7 screens
Different ages of the earth collapse
Into the present   Man!
Once there was a bridge of ice
To cross to a new land
Change fuels change
Dengue fever treks north with other viruses
From tropical environments
The travails of materiality count on language
The planet has a temperature, 3.5 Celius degrees higher
Spells "kaput" for business as usual

Sonnet for Gray

Gray walks into the room with a suitcase of raindrops. Marge
looks up from her bookkeeping to study a sentence scaling the
wall like a spider. Jack, the linguist, views the arachnid through
a magnifying glass. "It has one too many adjectives on one leg!"
he exclaims. Gray opens the suitcase. A chandelier of raindrops
brightens the room. Their boss falls asleep in a vision of feathers.

Gray likes the painting on the wall. It could be a sunset inside a
matchbox, a hand grenade of gumdrops or a null set of footprints
in a green forest. The painting belongs to Marge. "I'll give you
a raindrop for it," Gray says. "I don't talk with colors," she
responds, juggling a handful of adjectives. Jack opens a window,
marvels at the paragraph of trees on fire with beauty.

Gray closes the suitcase and imagines its mind is a cloud.
Feathers float to the street on a pillow of words.

image of white and blue

become nothing
abominable mind whisper
deer dark breath voyage up nibbled bark
water flute rock notes
ravine throat
silent ripple echoes
where to place you
in landscape
diamond flesh
cold feet hallucination
China cliff illusion
distraught branches
ermine covered
bird balanced
Basho tongued

first snow
ivory barge of sky sea
succulent cloud waves
thigh white
chip
flake
free fall
touch with nipple step
wind-rouged face
pulled by skin roots
into blood crests
spruce blue eye watch
thin needle crescent sight
night threads frail phosphorus

vivid sun birthday
suddenly
womb shudder
placenta drops of light on blue horizon
blue glow widens
dominates
spectral memory sequence
warm vaporous
before walk
breasts shimmered blue at lip fall
slow moving bergs of silk ice
mouth brain crystals
fusion touched

SONNET FOR BLUE

Blue draws a horse and saddles dawn with a sapphire.
A jeweler explains a sapphire is a corundum made
of aluminum and oxygen. His wife, Jane, owns a cat
with blue eyes that loves opera. Mozart had blue eyes
when he composed the two acts of *The Magic Flute*.
Though, there is some debate about his eyes.

Blue paints a flying horse and soars above the plains
of consciousness. Deep inside the earth, intense heat
creates sapphires. Cerulean requests Mozart's
The Magic Flute at dinnertime. The jeweler offers
20% off blue diamonds and 50% off Cerulean.
Blue sketches a waterfall of oats for the horses.

Blue stars are the hottest ones that exist.
Blue creates a barn of blue stars in the sky.

BLACK DOG'S FANCY

I was another person – the sea
flooded my eyes, rocks,
shells and seaweed deposited
in the hollows of the mind.
Salt leaked into the arteries of my heart.
I walked across the sand dune
of lost identity, clues buried
in what was no longer there.
Clouds meandered in a braggadocio
of forms; the wind spoke in tongues.
Fish dove in and out of my blood.
Seabirds fed on random thoughts.
Sunlight transfigured my flesh
into a prism of space.
I joked about death – the world
reduced to a spray of ashes
in a cosmic sea.
Selves collided into one.
In a frenzy, a black dog leapt
into green waves.

SONNET FOR GREEN

Green edges time to a glass cliff, dawdles in the grass
for the rest of the day. Meanwhile, Maybelline paints
her fingernails and toenails green, devours a bowl
of guacamole and texts her love interest, Max, on her
smartphone. "Time haywire; threatens suicide" He
texts back: "Dig, babe. Time split an hour ago."

Max reads Whitman and drops green windowpane acid.
Time shivers, then leaps from the glass cliff into a buoyant
timelessness. Meanwhile, Maybelline dyes her hair green,
plays some Chuck Berry and answers her smartphone.
"O, Maybelline, time didn't make it," Scam Likely says.
Gleefully, Max hangs with his Mexican green conure.

Green plots with trees to reclaim the earth.
Creator issues the Green Commandments.

assignment on waking

the argument of painted shoes
rejects the jargon of the master

bells ring

the paragraph walks on stage

the litany begins

soft monsters fold flowers into balls

the solar system yellows

on cue the future shines
on the alphabet highway

all rise

the judge disrobes
and judgments haunt
the stalled philosopher of manners

roll over enjambments
trick the dead line into life

so this is consciousness
of the dance
whirlwind of tiny kisses transmitted
by a savior of mild confusion

off goes the editing button

the child of busted alarms
resists the punishment

TOO

a hurricane of numbers forged on syntactical darkness

just when you think
connections bounce off

the shoulders of giants
the phone rings
the stew in the pot grows cold

Hurry up honey, the rambling typist
promised the interview committee
a session of colons by dawn!

consistency is the verdict of small minds

aphorisms grow shutters
when windows relinquish
the meaning of light

caught in the rhythm of dissonance
the revised stare enhances
shadows

empty institutions flitter away
rules of mind ease up

Sonnet for Yellow

A black cat's yellow eyes consume darkness.
Marilyn, proprietor of *Smart Hair & Nails*, styles
blond hair into a honeycomb of artificial intelligence.
Amber fragments of dreams confound narrative.
Brett, Marilyn's lover, brushes his flaxen teeth
with Brillo and calls in sick at *Drones & Things*.

Marilyn wears hot pants to a school board meeting
on banned books, causing a mass hysteria of bananas.
Forsythias bloom in divots of mind.
Brett, suffering nuclear indigestion, speeds through
a caution light and nails Chick-fil-A crossing the road.
Iowa and Florida ban the most books from schools.

A gold brush of leaves swipes the sky.
The sun blushes lemons.

Red Ink on a Timeless Day

The mind, insatiable pipsqueak, beat it
through a hole in an empty sky
after a battleship of generalities lobbed
an artillery shell of French pastries at it
It made no sense
But what could ( ) do
Consider tv news for a moment
the unending brutality and stupidity
of Homo Sapiens
with their happy prescription drug commercials
between bleeding lead stories
Que faisons-nous pour changer cela
Not much
So, ( ) went for a stroll
through a forest of rogue ideas
But sans mind, inevitable con artist,
( ) couldn't make sense of them
as they babbled and drooled
from the mouths of marionettes and rabid dogs
Being partial to partiality
( ) exited the forest in a rainstorm of taxis
caught one to the nearest bar
After four or five of my favorite libations
( ) left the joint with a woman
who savored sucking on lifesavers
during acts of love
By the time ( ) returned home
( ) found the mind, incorrigible hustler,
at my desk

revising and editing this poem
The bastard employed a harsh red pen
slashing some real gems
like this one:
A ruby train barreled down rusted tracks
during a soothsayer carnival
in a hayloft of disinformation
That's bad ass
( ) told the mind, inveterate crybaby,
just as it struck ( ) from the poem
with its temperamental pen

SONNET FOR RED

Red sends the Queen of Hearts a bouquet of roses and a love letter.
Dear Queenie, My heart belongs to you. Dump the king. Regards,
Anonymous. Jack plays another game of solitaire before feeding
his pet cardinal, Marvelous. Roses dig a judicious amount of coffee
grinds and Epsom salt in their soil. Consuming too many beets,
may cause temporary paralysis of the vocal cords. Queen faints.

Due to the way the wavelengths of photons stretch, the apparent
redshift of stars indicates an expanding universe. Marvelous's mates
protect their turf and attract lovers with their songs. The Queen of
Hearts encourages the King of Hearts to stick a sword in his head.
"It's over," she says. "I'm in love with an anonymous lover."
Jack makes a beet smoothie and attempts to sing like Marvelous.

Whoit Whoit Whoit Whacheer Whacheer.
Red raiment is racy.

6

FUSION

The emptiness of a beautiful day
Crawls into bed with me.
Stars in the yard play kickball
With the moon.
Moon prefers monkey-in-the-middle
With asteroids named Ursula and Smoke.
My mind sits at a table
With a clock minus hands.
It has captured my knights and bishops.
My queen is drunk in a mirror of regret.
Sleep writes a letter to a lover in a foreign country.

Hello! How have you been? Why is the grass
Still green in the fall of autumn's leaves?
I like maple red leaves and chocolate milkshakes.
The last book I read was made of diamonds
And seashells. I stood on my head
In an ocean wave until the library called
For the book's return. Please write me.
I wear your stolen necklace, Love.

A stray brick in the front yard complains
Of constipation and the solitary life
Of an object separated from it buddies.
I used to have wisdom teeth, rode my bike
through snowstorms to get to work.
Did I mention my vision of a planet
With possibilities, orbiting a yellow sun
That paints the sky blue or any color on its palette.
My heart used to be gray
Until it burst into a rainbow.

DRUTHERS

Too much about the world, Frank watered his knees with a common
garden hose. "This much is for certain," Frank said, thinking of the
Uncertainty Principle and relishing the hotdog moment of talking to
himself during a foolish and awkward scene in front of his neighbors
and some dogs, gawking or sniffing about on this very warm day in
late winter, due to global warming according to some, while others
were firmly camped in the wicked behavior of El Niño's above average
ocean surface temperatures or something like that now that the Internet
was broken (is too!). And Frank who would have loved to checkout
precisely the facts about El Niño's effect on atmospheric temperature on
the Net because for as certain as the *Uncertainty Principle* allows, which
for Frank meant something about the speed of his sneakers in the olden
days, like how fast they transported him to the hoop and back, and
in doing so, lost all sense of place, and the screaming fans of his (oh,
Frank had many fans) clocked in their minds seconds of splendiferous
hang-time in the *Ether of Now Where Am I*, like some Mississippi River
paddle-boat captain lost in a reverie of waves in his own brand of pure
motion and the absence of place. As if on this side of the equation (the
one moving fast as hell), New Orleans with all its charming anomalies,
would never gel again into delta magnificence but fly forever like some
rigged Zeno's arrow through motionless space, which Frank, having his
druthers, called a real drag, considering the beauty of earth at any given
moment.

In Praise of Cats

Today is yesterday.
What has happened to a morning
Of birdsong and whimpers of love?
I'm here and not here
in the chess game of thought –
pawn of light in the subtle darkness,
snared player in the gambit of time.
I know a cat named Poe
that stalks a celestial garden.
The mind discloses truth.
Verse ends with a trumpet
in a traffic jam of jazz.

Yesterday is today.
The world doesn't have to be treated
like a garbage can of lies.
It's just birds and feathers.
Love's heartache wrapped
in a litany of second chances,
battered cello in harmony with the moon.
I know a cat named Bogie
that dines with a clowder of angels.
The mind bleeds justice.
Verse ends with a web of imagery
in rafters of illusion.

Today is tomorrow.
Night arrives in a stolen convertible.
A woman opens a bottle of whiskey
to conduct an orchestra of shadows.

We met on a pilgrimage to ecstasy.
I know a cat named Cleo
that purrs a drowsy eternity.
The mind enshrines freedom.
Verse ends with an equation
for a prayer on the lips
of a kiss.

A POEM FOR KEN IRBY

As for metaphysics, cross the bridge
of something into nothing
Wind howls in the mind of what is not there
In the dance of quarks
the garden we wish to behold
is hidden
Go there in words –
each one a light detector
for what is real

Hours before, I walked down East Main Street
In Gloucester   alone with a smartphone
tracking my steps – I survived a storm of hats
and wayward signs until the harbor
settled into a bronze of fishing boats,
green and yellow lobster traps – some
with plants looped through them like Jerry Garcia
ties and sheltered by a sky wafting   pink

I was waiting for
a poetry reading in Ferrini's
old home to begin
On a neighbor's roof
a seagull squawked
at my passing steps
as the moon rose –
a super self
resting in a nearby tree
preening
associations
offered

We're moving into cold   again
though leaves in trees
still smitten with summer
hesitate to offer their dying colors
I didn't know the poet
Friends, colleagues and former students
arrived to celebrate him and remember
his life and words

Once the door opened
I became a firefly in the darkness
of a hieroglyphic notebook –
thoughts on Olson's projective verse – how
Irby shaped words – the speech of the
man himself
in his all-encompassing being
gifted into lines
of geography   memory   stories
around endless tables
details of love and loss
passion and   absence
placed on pages –
streams of syllables like polished stones
running   above
          under
and through the chapel of understanding
gnosis of the moment
in the whirlwind   of space
and time

GLINT OF PROPHECY

My work extends into
And far past the hiccups of revelation
If there were such a thing as a "moment" ago
I would file my claim of excessive ice-melt with the proper authorities
Turn right at the next hiatus

There is always room for invention and caged techniques
When chasing history around the block
The motive for a black eye eludes my intention
You say: "Toss me an avocado."
So, I do

Like all of us in the literary trade
Poesy is under a lot of pressure
Should we laugh now and outright
Those in power banter back and forth
During the Powerless Parade

After the unlawful seizure of my socks
I agree to the terms on making sense
Those who protest the construction
Of a House of Metaphor in their neighborhood
Look uneasy in the brilliant sunlight

I am thinking of light
Solar power and the dawn of a new age
Everything shakes to be new
A honey of mine reminds
My uncombed mind.

Innovate as Necessary

A replenishment of ideas challenged the forecast

"You're cute," she said, and left with my umbrella.

"Swimmingly," the brain researcher announced.
"A virtual habitat completed in near record time."

So many genetic options and features

I took the rhythm of sentences as a mandate
Stoked hysteria with provocative syntax

We stayed together until flags disappeared
Changed the future

Didn't we

Dear Diary,

If the Creator is nothingness,
then we're in for a surprise
when matter and energy vape
to their source.

      Today is blue sky with one cloud
          in the shape of a white whale.
             It's hard not to think of Melville
                seeing a mountainous whale
                  outside his study.
                    So, I do.

Weather is cool
    crisp
    with
    a
    slight
    slap
    in
    the face.

          Though shadows of me and my dog
         are causal and relaxed on an asphalt road.

I'm not sure where the people who live in the various houses are as the
earth tumbles along in its misery and joy. I don't believe I am in a ghost
town as a sharp pain passes through my head as if one thought were
sharpening another, creating a spark for others to follow in the shape of
a waterfall or an ocean hugging a distant horizon, flashing purple smoke
signals to a capsized boat.

Distraction is a hobby of mine,
walking my dog is a charm bracelet.

Just this morning, I found the charm for a robin,
the real one in my eyes, hopping down a sidewalk
speckled with points of light. Then a white crocus
flower appeared and the avant-garde of spring
enlivened my steps.

I'm lucky to be loved
by those who love me
and do my best
to love them back.

It's always been about love.
I'm
sure
the
void
digs
that.

BLUE FEET

On the canvas
Of eyelids

The dancer is
Snowflake piano

Welcome to the new
Calendar of hearts

If the message
Is sunlight

Through windows
Cry orange holiday

With a voice
Trickling ice

Sesame

for Peter Kidd & Kerry Zagarella

We size the world to fit our problems
In schools, teachers
Demand order in the minds
Of children

           No leaping

                    No frogs or myths

Up the sleeve

That is why I am a post-post-expletive-modern
Card-carrying member of the star commune
I eschew preordained commands
The sky is pink

           No, it's purple

                    Now blue – trembling

Like a pair of green lips

That must mean it's time for red wine
Fine cigars with friends
leaning against the custom fenders
Of silver machines

Let's go somewhere
Cruise up and down an unpaved thought
Park our eyes on a cosmic anomaly
Patch out on ribbons of hard rain
Come to a screeching halt

                    Make believe

Hello, my name is Santa Claus

What's your

I've deposited your requests

In a sea of hidden treasures

Where they swim with the ghosts of pirates

                                        And Flying fish

That is why it snows and my beard

Is wonderfully white

Twinkle twinkle…

Mystery is the portal in every star

Open

Sesame

DESTINATION

The brain is a country
Without a flag
Some days it is formless
Though prefers to work
With a clay of forms

        Ensconced in darkness
        It strikes matches
        Throughout the day
        And far into the night

      At its center is
      A treasure map
      Of galaxies

Flowers bloom
In the brain
Thoughts don
Colorful robes
Parade with animals
And insects

        It cloaks identity during
        Telepathic conversations
        With sea mammals
        And tiny fish

The brain is waterfall
Of concepts and constructs
Hosts the Carnival
Of Nothingness
On an annual basis

For inspiration it envisions
Orchards of timelessness
In a paradise of atoms
May open
The encyclopedia
Of childish tricks

A confidant of the body
It orchestrates journeys
Of transcendence
And immanence
On a reliable schedule
To where it must go

7

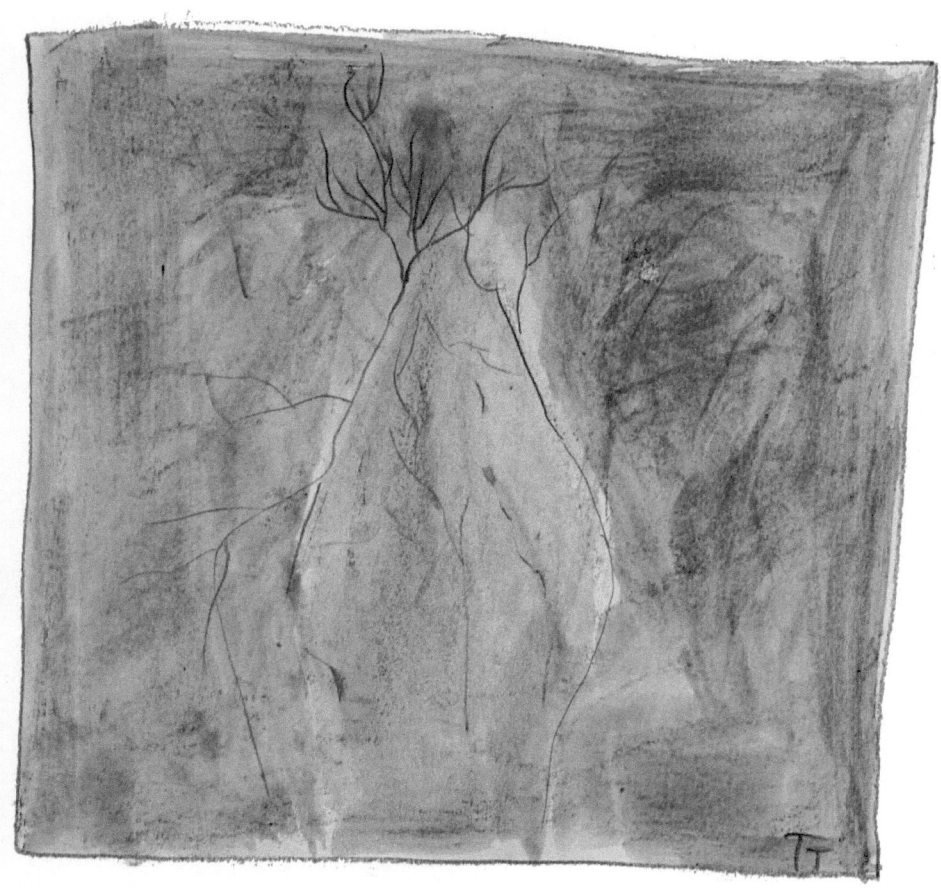

Mountaintop of Mirrors

The world is violet, peony, crocus.
My name is Tulip.
I sleep in the embrace of trees
that live in the wind with shadows
and ghosts, playing with thunder
and lightning bolts.

Remember Mt. Olympus?
Remember the gods/goddesses toying with your mind?
Remember your pagan childhood?

The world is rose, dahlia, lilac.
My name is Aster.
I come from nowhere with a message
in an empty bottle.
It's a lovely day of ocean waves and clouds.
Seagulls sail the sky.

Remember getting drunk on the beach?
Remember meteors sparkling in your eyes?
Remember the smile on your face?

The world is phlox, poppy, daisy.
My name is Marigold.
Life is here for the purpose of being here.
In the depth of its rocky bones,
death is a flea of time, nothing more.
Every grand civilization disappears.

Remember when you were here?
Remember when you were not?
Remember when you were again?

The world is cosmos, petunia, iris.
My name is Wisteria.
I imbibe rain offered to me.
My portable cross is made of matchsticks.
I'm a flame,
lighting bug in a jar of night.

Remember the days of nuclear love?
Remember the cold isolation of being alone?
Remember the welcomed retreat into solitude?

The world is zinnia, larkspur, begonia.
My name is Hydrangea.
I survive in various ideologies of soil –
capitalism, socialism, fascism, communism.
I'm weary of wars and stolen lands.
The dirt of earth is my mother and mirror.

Remember reaching the mountaintop of mirrors?
Remember the beautiful reflection of nothing at all?
Remember the All?

The world is primrose, bluebell, columbine.
My name is ...

PROCEDURE

Extract imagination   rinse down
with the logic of responsibility   wrap in mediocrity
Cauterize brain wound by asking 50 friends
and associates or those who have found
something troubling about your personality
to revoke their rights to the Fifth Amendment
Next   place the imagination in a gold cage
with the New York Times Best Seller: *Infectious Tips*
for Waste Management Managers   followed by the classic
Why CEO's Make More Than You
Return to normalcy guaranteed
within ten to fifteen days   if not
binge watch the evening news with earplugs
Any questions

Rural America

The wolf in the white tuxedo will pick you up
in a baby blue Bonneville convertible
with white-wall tires. Top forty hits on the radio.
Legend dictates he was born in Montparnasse,

offspring of a mother with a transcendental ego,
shock of purple hair and ballet slippers
on her ivory feet. Dad lugged a postal bag
through Parisian streets, a copy of Paul Eluard's

Liberté in it, along with a gold watch
and a bag of peanuts.
Not much has been verified about the wolf,
other than his predilection for magic.

Simple stuff really: molding a lump of clay
into a blue sky; twisting a cloud into a saxophone
or zoo animal; turning virtual stock trades
into a convention of rabbits in an empyrean meadow.

The press maintains that he came to America
after his mother identified as a celestial angel.
Dad chose a field of poppies as his final resting place.
He's been accused of making up his own biography:

*I'm just a kid from rural America, played football
and badminton in high school. Smoked a pack a day.*
A little black dress is more than suitable
for drinks and a night on the town.

Rumor has it that he's quite the lover.
Seems passion stimulates his spirituality.
Is love the only God?
Go ahead and ask him.

Count on him to be the upmost gentleman.
Despite all the misinformation about him,
he attends the Church of Electric Body and Soul
on a semi-annual basis.

When he howls, the dark side of the moon
descends into the ocean's imagination.
His form of prayer lights the candle of perception.
Though accused of apostasy, his heart beats truth.

ACCELERATION

As thought requires
Race into an incomprehensible
Stable position

Press face to sea
See gull
Or simple shell

In the entrails of words
Love bids omen
The sky cloaks dark energy

Did you say road or object
The exhaust of memory or telegram
Of remorse to the wrong address

Fill out the intrusive questionnaire
On spacetime –
Ineluctability of mind's equations

I too am lost in superlatives for now
The speed of what to say
And how to say it

SUBTLE INTRUSION

I went for a walk, bumping into a mermaid along the way.
It was a rather cold day; my nose froze bright red and popped
into my hand like a red rubber ball. I had lots of fun playing jacks
with a red rubber ball with my kid brother, Marvin. Assume;
I suffered a childlike break from reality when the mermaid spoke:
"Hey, Hal, why not come in for a swim with me. I have
an extra set of gills." I looked at my watch to check the time.
It ticked my blood pressure was too high; I needed to eat
more fruits and vegetables; someone had hacked my mind.
The mermaid's emerald tail tattooed my eyes with beauty.
"Aren't you cold in this weather?" I asked. "What weather?"
she said, diving into a snowbank. I studied her exit strategy
as if it were a book filled with entertaining facts: *In zillions and
zillions of years the universe will vanish until it realizes it
was never here. Then things will begin again.* No ordinary
snowbank, I deduced, dipping a hand into serene water,
before I took the plunge.

ABRASIONS

*

Saxophonists improvise with dogs
Barking in somnolent neighborhoods.
Molecules adopt erotic forms
During pink sunsets.
Cigarette butts in the street
Foster esoteric insights.
Say grandfather now and grow quiet.
Time is old/mind ticks.
Birds chirp atomic numbers.
In a vat of emptiness,
the cosmos ignites.

*

What can be done?
Philosophers grasp chaos
And leap from bridges.
Televisions go blank
With promises.
It is time to focus eyes
On the palette of galaxies,
Accept an absent future
As the present, strap
Memories to helium balloons,
Salute heretics on the loose.

*

A hawk floats above a gorge.
Apple trees blossom.
X times spacetime, the soul
Pops into visible reality
Like a rabbit out of a hat.
Oh, Atman!
Crows clip hemlocks with black wings.
Spiders crawl across imported bananas.
Forgiveness mirrors heaven
When blind drunk.
Who will save the planet?

*

Eyes revere the sun.
Insight into a sentence
Is the sentence.
Death haunts life
Like a family of doppelgängers.
Without smartphones,
We could call and answer
Each other with silence.
Some question the existence
Of a material world.
Atoms shelter eternity.

*

As narration begins
Votive candles burn
In halls of apology.
Semiotic bandits rob
Signs of meaning.
AI deep fakes reality
Into a virtual coma.
Conspiracies replace
Knowledge.
Hate edges love.
Heart beats lonely.

*

The absence of government
Should signal the end
Of impulse shopping.
Here's one:
If men take 200-300 milligrams
Of vitamin C per day,
They could live an extra six years.
Women can expect an extra year
With the same dose.
Take time to visualize
A splendid world.

Beep

Through the moon's binoculars,
I watch as her body emerges
In the midst of a fantasy.
Now, I leap across a blank page
in a synaptic whirlwind of ink.

So many questions.
What's up with my mind?
What if wore a hat of daffodils
Or burned like yellow candles
Of forsythia on a hillside?

I want to infiltrate, bond
With the heart of love,
On a day the sun parades down
The street in flashy sneakers.
Maybe, join the procession of dogs

Sniffing spring, green trees.
Romance serenades time.
In the long sigh of what comes next –
Footprints etched in wisps of sand.
There is a storm of resurrected ghosts

In my eyes, a halo of desire
Stapled to my head.
I duck in and out of her smile,
Reside in the insensibility
Of the unknowable,

Blow across a veiled sky
In a jeep of clouds.
With a horn, improvising,
On the temperament of love
And beauty.

While Trapped in a Blanket

In the crosshairs of dilemma & ecstasy
I fell asleep inside an alarm clock
That happened during my winter mood
When snowstorms stalked the imagination
Of the piano man
& beer flowed freely
Down the street

To my chagrin someone stole my snooze button
& took off with my wife to Honolulu
I sneezed a series of volcanic eruptions
Until a whiplash of windows emitted
A cold wind
With strung-out birds
& their lawyers

Feeling somewhat distraught
I called the Surrealist Hotline for help
The counselor-on-call advised me to never use
The word "surreal" in casual conversations
Or to describe anything
Slightly akimbo
To reality

"Akimbo" stuck in my throat
Like a chicken bone
My mother always said
Check your poems for bones
Regardless of energy source
Intent

Meaning

With the real world pressing my pants and long-sleeve shirt
I placed the playground of language & mind
Back in its game box downed a coffee and raced to work
Through a maze of red lights
With sirens blaring
In the microphones
Of my ears

Ballast

1

Attached to reality
By conceits of imagination
Pound form into being
High-velocity hits result in ocean
Stellar maps and street names
Maple Lark
Mozart
Beethoven
We've been told
Let go in the wind
Instruct

2

Feathers and wings
Sky distant
But cozy
Engines made of wax
Reverse works
Walking down the street
Praise gravity
The weight
Of ants
Whisper to earth
We're back

LAUGHTER AND TEARS

This morning
the sun arrived
with a bouquet
of flowers on fire,
it's belly red with roses.
But I'm not sure
of windows or mirrors.
I might have been ten
years older now or so
short I needed heel lifts
and an ache in my side,
as if my stomach had
reached its capacity
for angry fish.

Things matter
but then I forget where
I placed my snowshoes,
my book of memories,
your name before
you change it. Why
even green bananas
filed for divorce from
the rest of the groceries.
It's difficult to make sense
in these days of oligarchs
and billionaires running
rampant in the Ice Age
of the moment.

.

Thank the Lord
I'm addicted to the lure
of winks and ambience.
The perfumed hair
of a woman whizzing
by me on a motorcycle
of tattoos, dreamy smell
of misspelled words
in a bottle of regrets.
The balm of ocean
on sandy feet.
The this and that
we call ourselves
in subtle darkness.

Please hear me.
I'm the narrative living
next door to you.
I've shaved my head
and splashed my cheeks
with primary colors.
I'm ready for something.
If you guess what that is,
please call me or hit a baseball
through my picture window.
I'm at home or will be.
Believe me, whittling
myself into subliminal shapes
of laughter and tears.

Joel Dailey

RICHARD MARTIN is a past recipient of the National Endowment for the Arts Literature Fellowship for Poetry, founder of the Big Horror Poetry Series (Binghamton, New York, 1983-1996) and a retired Boston Public Schools principal. He lives in the city with his family and pets.

www.ingramcontent.com/pod-product-compliance
Lightning Source LLC
Chambersburg PA
CBHW020402130626
46549CB00006B/2409